IT'S TIME TO EAT BEETS

It's Time to Eat BEETS

Walter the Educator

Silent King Books
A WhichHead Entertainment Imprint

Copyright © 2024 by Walter the Educator

All rights reserved. No part of this book may be reproduced in any manner whatsoever without written per- mission except in the case of brief quotations embodied in critical articles and reviews.

First Printing, 2024

Disclaimer

This book is a literary work; the story is not about specific persons, locations, situations, and/or circumstances unless mentioned in a historical context. Any resemblance to real persons, locations, situations, and/or circumstances is coincidental. This book is for entertainment and informational purposes only. The author and publisher offer this information without warranties expressed or implied. No matter the grounds, neither the author nor the publisher will be accountable for any losses, injuries, or other damages caused by the reader's use of this book. The use of this book acknowledges an understanding and acceptance of this disclaimer.

It's Time to Eat BEETS is a collectible early learning book by Walter the Educator suitable for all ages belonging to Walter the Educator's Time to Eat Book Series. Collect more books at WaltertheEducator.com

USE THE EXTRA SPACE TO TAKE NOTES AND DOCUMENT YOUR MEMORIES

BEETS

It's time to eat, it's beet time now,

It's Time to Eat

Beets

Pulled from the dirt, fresh from the plow.

Round and red with leafy tops,

Beets are ready for yummy chops!

In the ground, they like to hide,

Bright and purple, deep inside.

We wash them clean and cook them right,

Beets are such a tasty sight!

They're earthy sweet with colors bold,

Purple, red, and even gold!

When you slice them, what a treat,

Pretty circles of yummy beet!

You can roast them, warm and sweet,

Or slice them raw for a crunchy treat.

Add some salt or eat them plain,

Beets bring joy again and again.

It's Time to Eat

Beets

Beet juice stains your hands bright pink,

A magic color, don't you think?

Little fingers, red and neat,

Just from touching tasty beets!

Some say beets taste like the earth,

Full of flavor, full of mirth.

They're good for us, with vitamins strong,

A healthy snack that lasts so long!

Beets can go in salads too,

With greens and cheese and veggies true.

Or mashed up smooth, in a big red spread,

Beets bring color to our bread!

A beet can be a funny treat,

With a taste that's earthy, soft, and sweet.

It makes us smile, it makes us chew,

Beets are fun for me and you!

So if you're brave and want to try,

A beet is here—no need to be shy!

With every bite, it's something new,

It's Time to Eat

Beets

A veggie treat that's good for you.

So let's dig in and take a bite,

Beets are here, fresh and bright!

Round and red and fun to eat,

Hooray for healthy, tasty beets!

ABOUT THE CREATOR

Walter the Educator is one of the pseudonyms for Walter Anderson. Formally educated in Chemistry, Business, and Education, he is an educator, an author, a diverse entrepreneur, and he is the son of a disabled war veteran. "Walter the Educator" shares his time between educating and creating. He holds interests and owns several creative projects that entertain, enlighten, enhance, and educate, hoping to inspire and motivate you. Follow, find new works, and stay up to date with Walter the Educator™ at WaltertheEducator.com

www.ingramcontent.com/pod-product-compliance
Lightning Source LLC
LaVergne TN
LVHW010622070526
838199LV00063BA/5241